IMAGES OF ENGLAND

Around Maghull
and Lydiate

LIVERPOOL ROAD MAGHULL

Once upon a time Maghull was a peaceful village where friends could calmly stand in the road to pass the time of day without a care in the world.

IMAGES OF ENGLAND

Around Maghull and Lydiate

John K. Rowlands

NONSUCH

First published 1997
This new pocket edition 2006
Images unchanged from first edition

Nonsuch Publishing Limited
The Mill, Brimscombe Port,
Stroud, Gloucestershire, GL5 2QG
www.nonsuch-publishing.com

Nonsuch Publishing is an imprint of Tempus Publishing Group

British Library Cataloguing in Publication Data.
A catalogue record for this book is available from the British Library.

ISBN 1-84588-296-2

Typesetting and origination by Nonsuch Publishing Limited
Printed in Great Britain by Oaklands Book Services Limited

Contents

TRAVELLERS' REST, MAGHULL.

The Travellers Rest at Hall Lane Bridge was demolished in 1936 and one of its landlords, Denis Clarke, is reputed to have travelled far abroad. It is said that he had been a coachman to the Czar of Russia and had received a golden whip for his services.

Introduction

In recent years I have been asked several times by students to help them in their researches into the social and commercial development of Maghull and Lydiate. It would appear that Maghull is a classic example of a country village developing into a town whilst Lydiate has generally maintained its rural charm. The main influence upon Maghull was the development of the ancient road from Liverpool to Preston into a turnpike, the building of the canal and then the arrival of the railway.

During the early nineteenth century many substantial houses were built for successful businessmen and merchants, many of whom, such as Frank Hornby and Isaac Roberts, gained international recognition. Moss Side Hospital and the Maghull Epileptic Homes have had a major influence upon British medicine and Maghull can make a claim to having held the first Grand National horse race. Famous poets and authors have lived here and, following the boom in house building after the last war, it became the home of several famous professional footballers as their status increased. The rich fields were a vital source of produce for Liverpool but it was a hard life for the farm labourer and it was in Maghull that the local farmworkers' strikes of 1913 started.

During the war the area gave safety to many families. Originally a place of refuge to those escaping from the Liverpool *Blitz*, they were followed by evacuees from all over the country and finally from around the world who, during their evacuation, lived in camps built in Maghull.

Sadly many of the fine halls and houses have been destroyed and there are relatively few original cottages remaining. However, amongst its treasures are the Scotch Piper Inn, Lydiate Hall, Lydiate Abbey, Maghull Manor House and Maghull chapel, all of which have been renovated in recent years.

The district has a rich history. This book describes the life in Maghull and Lydiate as villages and later, townships, as the twentieth century changed them. I hope it encourages others to seek out and record this history before it is lost forever.

Deyes Lane, c. 1941. A group of nurses of the Civil Nursing Reserve outside St Andrew's School.

One

Around the Township

Sandy Lane, Lydiate. A fairy tale cottage that our imagination hankers for could also conceal a difficult life of poverty and squalor.

Left: Lydiate Hall, *c.* 1895. George Bamforth Harrison of Toxteth visited Lydiate with his new wife and took this photograph of the porch into the Great Hall; he is the first known local photographer. It is thought that Lawrence Ireland built Lydiate Hall in the mid-sixteenth century as a quadrangular building. The stone from the oldest part, the demolished east wing, may now be part of the nearby farm shop run by Brian Sephton. Some superb wooden panels from the hall are now preserved in a house at Little Crosby.

Below: Our Lady's church, Lydiate, *c.* 1920. The meadow in front of the church, still with the steeple which was demolished in the 1930s, suggests the derivation of the name of Lydiate. 'Hlid-Geat' meaning swing-gate implies a gate or enclosure to stop grazing cattle from straying. The symbol is now incorporated in Lydiate's coat of arms.

Southport Road, c. 1905. The first building was Lydiate Post Office run by Mrs Bell, the eldest daughter of St Thomas's School's headmaster; Miss Mabel Holme recalls visiting the shop when walking home from school. The cottage is now called Holmbridge, which was the name of the adjacent Lollies Bridge in 1840. It is thought to be named after a cobbler who lived in a nearby thatched cottage – or perhaps it was the Mr Holme who was a local landlord in 1811.

Station Road, Lydiate, c. 1900. Rose Cottage is an excellent example of an agricultural worker's cottage and is still unspoilt. It backs onto The Croft behind the Scotch Piper Inn, which may explain its ancient link with the Moorcroft family. The ladies wearing the characteristic local bonnets, which are still occasionally seen today, are from left to right: Margaret Spencer, Mary Moorcroft and Bella Hooker.

Southport Road, c. 1900. This charming group of cottages at Sunny Side stood on the edge of Maghull Brook, behind the dog, which is the boundary between Lydiate and Maghull. In about 1921 Charles Bower bought an end cottage to start a small garage which was operated by Harry Johnson from 1947–1963. Three years later the buildings were demolished and replaced by the present filling station. The cottage on the left is thought to have been the home of Dr John Barnes who was born in Maghull and was a general practitioner in the area in the mid-nineteenth century before his early death.

Liverpool Road, c. 1960. Lydiate Mill and the miller's cottage were built in 1777 beside the former Liverpool to Preston turnpike, seen heading towards Aughton, and converted into a house in 1966. There was another windmill in Lydiate on the hillock behind Our Lady's church. Mill House Farm in Eggergarth was first mentioned in a 1298 deed concerning the diversion of Suddell Brook which still flows under the canal. The mill belonged to the Scarisbrick family until 1546, when it was sold to Laurence Ireland and three centuries later it passed to the Weld Blundells. The ruins of the water wheel remain.

Liverpool Road, *c.* 1910. The turnpike road climbed gently through the Oak Hill district of Lydiate which was surrounded by sandy lanes, thatched cottages and the intriguingly named Barrack Lane leading to the Barrack Cottages. Frank Bretherton, one of the most successful stage-coach proprietors in the North of England, built Oakhill House which is glimpsed through the trees on the right. The horses were changed from the coaches and stabled in the extensive buildings of Oakhill Farm opposite. The Revd Gibson suggested that Oakhill House may have been intended as an inn as it has the figure of a mitre on the balcony with the letters 'PD and P' *(Pro Deo and Patria* – For God and my Country). Dr Michael Heathcote, who was a general practitioner in Maghull for over forty years, died at Oakhill House in 1876. The next owner, Thomas Mather, a Liverpool corn merchant, sold Maghull Manor House which became the first Epileptic Home. The house later became a nursing home, offices for an insurance company and finally an electrical firm. It was demolished after the last war.

Liverpool Road North. My favourite photograph is one of the earliest of rural Maghull and it shows the distinctive slope of Liverpool Road North leading towards the Red Lion Bridge, behind the warehouse. The Red Lion Inn is seen as a much larger building and confirms the landlord's other occupation as a farmer. The spire of St Thomas's church, built in 1878, is not yet visible. There seems to be little evidence of road traffic and by the 1860s the turnpike was in decline, which suggests a possible date for the picture.

Red Lion Bridge, c. 1913. Tommy Barnes in the centre of his group of friends seemed to attract local photographers. By the 1920s the workers' houses on Liverpool Road had been converted into shops and businesses. The distant lorries are parked outside the British Workman's Cocoa Rooms beside Wadsworth's Wharf. The near houses, known locally as 'on the slope', had a wooden bridge leading from the footpath with Frampton's sweet shop next door. Other shops were Jackson's grocers, Mrs Chadwick's bicycle shop, a shoe shop, a saddlers, a bakery and Tom Harvey's garage.

Damfield Lane, c. 1962. Originally built as a William Deacon's bank, this small building near Red Lion Bridge became the offices of Maghull Parish Council from 1961, when opened by Sir Douglas Glover MP, until the present town hall was opened in 1984. It was then converted into a private dwelling. The neighbouring cottage had a public weighbridge outside and fees were taken through the small window overlooking the road.

Red Lion Bridge, c. 1930. Crossing Red Lion Bridge before a footpath was built in 1933 could be both dangerous and unpleasant; the small hut to the right was the Maghull mortuary and in 1926 the *Ormskirk Advertiser* complained that bus passengers could see inside the building. On the right are Cuckson's Cottages and the Salem chapel, built on land owned by George Cuckson of Race Course Farm in 1867. Methodist services were held there for a decade before the building was sold to Lancashire Education Committee to be used for teaching domestic science and woodwork to pupils from St Andrews' School and as a rest centre for evacuees during the *Blitz*.

Liverpool Road South, c. 1910. Mr Holden is seen resting whilst on his regular delivery round near an old turnpike milestone close to Red Lion Bridge. The woman is standing outside a small derelict cafe in what was formerly an important building in Maghull. It had been the Hare and Greyhound public house but was also the first post office in Maghull, situated beside the field called Male Green, the ancient centre of the township. The postmaster was a saddler, James Walkinson from Ashton-in-Makerfield, but his wife Elizabeth was born in Maghull.

Liverpool Road South. The impressive West House stood almost opposite Green Lane. It had been the first home in Maghull of Dr Frederick Gordon, a strong Irish personality who was born in Canada and who became perhaps the most fondly remembered general practitioner in the town. He eventually moved to High Pastures and Gordon Avenue is named after him. The postcard states that Ethel Swift was born at West House and married Stanley Sumner, a farmer who owned three farms, in about 1924. The house was demolished in the 1950s and replaced by a block of flats.

Damfield Lane, c. 1963. Although there were policemen living in Maghull from the 1840s, the first police station was established in Green Lane in 1870, with William Newsham from Preston and his family living there. Its replacement, an impressive building where the station sergeant lived, was demolished in 1963 to allow the widening of Northway. Temporary accommodation in huts near Northway Garage was arranged whilst the new police station was built near the new civic centre area, but it lacked the charm of its predecessor.

Damfield Lane, 1953. To commemorate the coronation in 1953, Maghull Parish Council proudly built the Coronation Garden behind the vicarage garden. Having a Yorkshire stone wall, bird bath, flowering shrubs and trees and flowers, it was a place of peace and beauty. Ten years later it was demolished for the dual carriageway. Behind the flag pole is the tithebarn. The Revd George Holden was Vicar of Maghull for over fifty years and with his father published the *Liverpool Tide Tables*. His important ecclesiastical library was bequeathed to Ripon Cathedral and the library is still greatly used.

Left: Hall Lane, Maghull, *c.* 1930. Maghull Hall stood on what is now Old Hall Field and was originally a large half-timbered sixteenth-century building. In 1805 the estate was sold for £7,800 to William Harper, whose daughter moved into the hall after marrying John Formby, the owner of Maghull race course where the first Grand Liverpool Steeple Chase was won in 1837 by The Duke. Bartholomew French, a ship owner and possibly related to Field Marshall French, bought the estate in 1858. From 1875 William Ripley, the manufacturer of Ripley Blue, lived there and between the wars the Boyer family took over the estate. The hall was demolished in about 1938.

Below: Northway, 1930. A land grant in 1230 described a forty-acre Maghull Wood at the southern boundary recalled by Woodend Farm, of which only the garden wall remains. The road to Liverpool led through the wood and in 1404, Robert Walsh was murdered there on his way to market. In 1861 Thomas and Margaret Ball worked the farm and in the space of a decade enlarged it by 100 acres, and their family to ten children. The farm would later be badly affected by foot and mouth disease and declined, before being demolished.

Station Road, Maghull, *c.* 1890. Jelly's Corner on the corner of Hall Lane and Station Road was named after John Jelly, a painter who lived in this house. His grandson Rafael Sabatini was born in Italy in 1875, but for a time lived here and attended a private school at Rose Dene in Liverpool Road South. He became a famous author writing historical novels including, *The Sea Hawk, Captain Blood* and *Scaramouche*, some of which became films starring Errol Flynn and Dame Flora Robson. He died in Switzerland in 1950.

The area partly bordered by Tailors Lane was known as Kennesse Green for over 500 years, but the arrival of the railway led to the building of several large houses. One house, Kennessee House, now demolished, was built in 1880 with an observatory by Isaac Roberts. He took several important photographs of stars and nebulae for which he gained international recognition and the Royal Astronmical Society's Gold Medal in 1895. Tailors Lane may have been named after the numerous tailors who had lived in the area; perhaps the tall imposing building on the far corner was part of the trade with workshops on the top floor.

Station Road, *c.* 1955. Maghull Station looks like a typical Hornby model railway level crossing with a signal box; could Frank Hornby have been influenced by it? The wooden porch next to Speake's newsagent shop was the entrance to Maghull Station sorting office and its distinctive postmark appears on many of the postcards used in this book. As part of a modernisation programme the signal box has been demolished and the gates replaced with barriers – and all of its charm has been lost.

Station Road, Maghull. Frank Hornby was already a successful toy manufacturer when he moved to The Hollies, the second house in this picture of 1908. The hedge surrounds the Lancashire and Yorkshire Railway Sports Field where Frank would watch games. As his company Meccano Ltd expanded he moved to Quarry Brook, but loaned the building in 1914 for use as a military hospital for Army Officers. After the First World War his two sons would often give local children rides in their cars. In 1929 Frank became the Unionist MP for Bootle. A diabetic, he died in the David Lewis Northern Hospital in 1936 and is buried in St Andrew's churchyard.

Two

Farming, Trades and the Professions

An everyday sight was the teamster and his horses travelling through the country lanes.

Green Lane, Maghull, *c.* 1890. Sitting in his trap outside Canal Farm is John Holme, who was born in Lydiate in 1848. John and his wife had a large family and many of their descendants still live in the area. The farm covered 50 acres and employed six men. On a summer's evening the family would sit on the balcony and enjoy the unbroken view across the Moss to Formby. Millicent Holme remembers her Grandmother Tickle, who took over the farm, handing out cakes and pies from the side window. The farm is now the Maghull Community Centre.

Clent Farm was first described in a 1376 land grant as 'Clente' but the original building may have been rebuilt in 1616. The Cropper family lived there from 1891 until the buildings were demolished in 1964. Robert Cropper was known locally known as the 'Onion King' because of the onions which were washed and in the farmyard where his grandson David is seen in 1948. David learned to drive in the Ford car which his father bought for £60 from Uncle Percy Adams after it had been in store during the Second World War. When Westway Medical Centre was being built on the site the duck stones forming the yard were uncovered.

Rosemary Farm, Downholland, c. 1890. Joseph Hurst and his wife stand with their family outside the farm. The family later moved to Lydiate and are still involved in farming. The men on the left are casual migrant Irish farm workers without whom the local farmers could not get the work done in busy seasons, especially the hay harvest. They lived in the 'Irishmen's house' or 'shants' built on the local farms. This was usually an old brick, one-storey building with a fire, a cold water tap or pump in the farmyard and chaff in bags for beds as the workers had to sleep on the floor. The 'shants' were very primitive and often in a filthy condition. Occasionally there was conflict with racial overtones between local and Irish labourers. However, by the 1890s Irish harvesters were becoming a scarce source of labour.

Downholland Hall was once described as a 'post and pattrel dwelling of mud and timber' built by the Holland family. In 1655 it was converted into a farmhouse and seems to have undergone major renovation in about 1890, revealing the rather flimsy floor seen here which does not appear to bother the workmen. The building has a magnificent flight of carved wooden stairs.

Charles Gard from Aughton met his future wife Martha, from Lydiate, at a Bible class and after marrying in 1914 they lived in Dodds Lane. Charles worked for the Pimbleys on Moss Side Farm and is seen standing here, around 1920, on the corner of Park Lane with a load of cabbages on his way to Cazenove Street Market in Liverpool, which was a vital outlet for the sale of local produce. He left the farm in 1930 to work in a Liverpool wine and spirits warehouse.

Frank Meadows of Lydiate bought the first threshing machine in the district and travelled as far as the North East looking for work. During the First World War there was great demand for extra food and any help to bring in the harvest was appreciated, including that of the many soldiers billeted in the district. Frank, who lived in a small cottage in Church Lane, was associated with the choir at St Thomas's church for fifty years.

Dick Dickinson, standing third from the left, had a small farm in Moss Lane, Maghull, and for a time had a contract with a canning firm in Liverpool to produce peas. During the short picking season he employed local hand pickers and it seems to have been a happy time, as shown in this 1950s photograph, with Dick's Ferguson tractor taking the workers home.

January and December 1940 were the coldest months for forty-five years and brought all transport to a halt. Booths, who had a farm near Sefton church, managed with some difficulty to deliver the milk to their regular customers in Maghull.

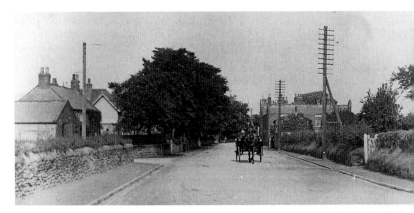

Liverpool Road South, 1914. When he first came to Maghull, Dr Frederick Gordon lived in West House, seen on the right. His practice covered a large area and he was driven on his rounds in an immaculate horse and trap by Bill Storrie who spent his whole working life with the doctor. Dr Gordon bought one of the first cars in Maghull, which was garaged beside the Hare and Hounds. On one occasion, whilst waiting for a confinement, Bill and the expectant father over-celebrated and Dr Gordon had to drive him home. The small building on the left was used to build coffins.

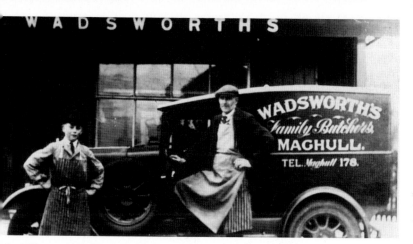

In 1880 teenager William Wadsworth moved from Northamptonshire to work with William Meadows, a butcher in Station Road. He later took over the business in Liverpool Road South started by the Shaw family in the 1840s. The horse delivery vans were replaced by a small fleet of motor vehicles after the First World War. Mr Cobham, who took over the business, is seen preparing for a delivery trip. The shop and adjacent post office closed down when Maghull Square opened and were replaced by Bryant House.

Tom Holden had a small grocer and chandlers shop on Liverpool Road North, from which he delivered to surrounding villages and farms. The business was continued by his son Dick and grandson Harold, and the shop is now occupied by Crays. Resting outside the Weld Blundell is Dick Heighway and his assistant. Tom Meadows was the landlord for thirty years until the late 1950s. The Holdens, who sold milk, grazed cows in Dr Gordon's field behind High Pastures. Tom died in 1947 aged 85 years, having attended the Methodist chapel since its foundation.

As the township grew there was a smithy in every part of Maghull. In 1854 Robert Barnes, a blacksmith, moved with his young family from Kirkby to Maghull to found the business which would be continued by his family for over a century. The Barnes' shop was behind the Maid of Erne public house in Liverpool Road North and is little changed from this photograph, with most of the original equipment still inside the workshop.

In the 1860s William Massey, a dental tooth manufacturer, moved from Hanley to Melling Lane. His dentist son, John, later built Kensington House, which became the Maghull Conservative Club in 1912; his initials are engraved on windows inside the porch. At the back of his home he built the small factory known as the Toothworks, which employed many local people until it was sold and demolished.

Mary Hunter (*née* Geldard) moved to Lydiate during the First World War to work for Dick Meadows at the Weld Blundell Hotel, where she met her future husband who was a teamster. She is seen in the backyard where Tom Meadows made baskets from the willow twigs grown behind with his apprentice, Eddie Allin, until 1927 when Eddie was made redundant at the end of his apprenticeship.

Liverpool Road South, c. 1908. The Liverpool to Preston turnpike was in existence from 1771 until 1877 and the Hare and Hounds hotel was built as a coaching inn. The farmers were dependant upon the Liverpool markets to sell their produce but there seems to have been a small market on the forecourt with produce on sale for local consumption.

Liverpool Road North. In the 1930s the Barnes family built a group of shops at the northern end of Maghull near their smithy. Mr Roberts had run the post office in Melling before opening a popular shop and the window display must have been very tempting to the children. The business is now Herbert Butler's the chemists. J. Halsall, the hairdressers next door, advertised having a qualified chiropodist in attendance.

Damfield Lane, *c.* 1950. A major landmark for canal and turnpike travellers for almost two centuries, the Red Lion hotel became a general store in 1910 and the last occupiers were the Rimmer family until it was demolished after the Second World War. A popular mooring point for barges, the 1881 census reports that John Broadhurst, the Master of *Kate*, his wife Mary Ellen the Mate, and their six small children tied up nearby. William, aged 11 years, was assistant crew member and at 8 years old, Alice was a nurse, which must have been a hard life.

Dover Road, 1951. The green fields of Maghull started to disappear during the 1930s when building began along the old turnpike road as the people of Liverpool looked for homes outside of the city. The Alt Estate was a major development planned to include a public house, shops and a cinema. Because of overcrowding in the local schools due to evacuees, two shops were opened as a school in 1941. Building restarted shortly after the war ended and one of the first private post-war houses built in Merseyside was No. 50 Gainsborough Avenue; in March 1946 Harold Wilson MP presented Mr and Mrs George Brice with a golden key.

Originally known as The Plough, the Weld Blundell landlords can be traced back to a Mr Holme in 1811, who was replaced by a Robert Fairclough in 1821. He and his son-in-law James Sumner would stay for over fifty years at the then New Lollie until about 1891, when it became the Weld Blundell Arms. William Pye is seen standing in the doorway with his family in about 1900; he was followed by Richard and Thomas Meadows until 1959 when Mrs Rigby became the landlady. Originally it had a tap room, a bar parlour and a living room.

> *In Loving Memory of*
> # 𝔚𝔦𝔩𝔩𝔦𝔞𝔪 𝔓𝔶𝔢,
> *The beloved husband of Ann Pye,*
> *who departed this life March 13th 1902,*
> *in his 72nd year,*
> *and was interred at St. Andrew's Church,*
> *Maghull.*

Before becoming a publican, William Pye lived in Neden's Row in Maghull and had a small wheelwright's business. He moved to the Weld Blundell in the 1880s and made coffins behind the pub. He built the row of ten small cottages on Southport Road that bears his name. William and Ann Pye still have many relatives living in the district. Sadly, Ann was to die only three months after her husband and she is buried beside him in St Andrew's churchyard.

Thomas Whalley, third from the left on the back row, worked as a farm labourer before becoming a boiler man at the Epileptic Homes. Farm workers generally lived-in with the farmers but by the 1870s, several cottages were built especially for them in Southport Road and their status changed from that of servant to day labourer. The first Lancashire branch of the farmworkers' union was formed at the Hare and Hounds and William Hutchinson, who was in charge of the pig herd at Dodds Farm, led the farmworkers' strike in 1913 when police had to escort food convoys through Maghull.

Southport Road. As war threatened the Universal Drum Company moved from Liverpool to Lydiate to escape the risk of air-raids and the manager lived in a house on the site. Tony Kelly and his wife Winifred were moved to Lydiate and lived on the site for over forty years. Millions of metal drums were collected from the docks and re-used after cleaning and repair, which was essential for the war effort. Recently the site was cleared and after some public concern about the previous use of the land, the Moorings Estate was built on it.

After demobilisation many local ex-servicemen sought work in the new, thriving factories in Aintree and Kirkby. Stan Beddows of Lydiate had served overseas in the Royal Air Force and started work as a driver at British Enka before leaving to work at Moss Side Hospital, another major local employer.

Three

Schools and Churches

St Andrew's church. The foundation stone of the church was laid on 2 July 1878 following the efforts of the Revd J.C. Leigh to replace the ancient Maghull chapel, which was built in the early thirteenth century.

REV. T. E. GIBSON

The Reverend Thomas Ellison Gibson, a distinguished local historian, was the priest at Our Lady's church, Lydiate, from 1860. He was born in Salford and attended Broadwood House boarding school in Maghull, first visiting Lydiate Hall in 1831. Gerard Manley Hopkins, the poet, stayed with the Lightbound family at Rose Hill Villa, Lydiate, in 1870 and was inspired by the tree-lined lanes of Lydiate to write *Spring and Fall*.

St Catherine's chapel, built in the early sixteenth century, was a private chapel for the Ireland family of Lydiate Hall and may be dedicated to John Ireland's mother, Catherine. The 'Abbey' as it is known locally, was derelict for centuries, as shown in this photograph taken by George Harrison in about 1895; there was also a private chapel in the hall.

Above: Our Lady's church, *c.* 1898. The foundation stone of Our Lady's church, the gift of Thomas Weld Blundell and designed by Mr J. Scott of London, was laid on 31 March 1853. Over the north door are the sculptured heads of the benefactor and his wife. The priest is the Revd E. Powell who spent seventeen years in Lydiate and is buried in the graveyard with other priests from the Society of Jesus.

Right: These serious young men are waiting to leave Our Lady's for the May Parade in about 1930. The lady at the back is Mrs Carberry, the headmistress, whose son John Thomas became a Roman Catholic priest in the Royal Air Force. Her sister, Mrs Haskayne, a farmer's wife from Station Road, stands at the side.

Southport Road. St Thomas's Church of England school was built by subscription in 1839 with the adjacent headmaster's house also being used by boarders. In 1854 George and Ann Ramsbottom ran the school; George was also an insurance agent and ran Lydiate Post Office from the school, which moved to new premises in Kenyon's Lane. The old school was demolished and replaced by the Shieling Care Home in 1987.

Mr Tyrer was headteacher at St Thomas's for over forty years before the First World War. His assistant Miss Wignall 'was a pleasant, tall, good looking lady with her hair always done on top'. He was also helped by his daughter Ann who left to teach at Maghull School before becoming headteacher at Wherwell in Wiltshire. The charming young lady at the front of this group in 1910 is unknown, but those recognised are Mildred Rothwell, Gladys Baybutt and Ernie Leatherbarrow.

Liverpool Road North. In about 1860 a Mr Chuck bought Woodland Mount in Liverpool Road North and Methodist services were held in a wooden hut in the gardens. Twenty years later the hut was moved to the site of the car park of the present chapel but the building, which had a whitewashed interior, shuttered windows and a felt roof, proved to be inadequate for the expanding group of worshippers. In 1895 the new chapel was opened at a cost of £1,128.

Station Road, Maghull, *c.* 1910. The first Roman Catholic services in Maghull were held in 1887 at Massey's Barn in Station Road and later in Colgan's Barn in Melling Lane before St George's church was built in 1929. The priest's house was erected in 1892. In later years I enjoyed the hospitality of the housekeeper, Mrs Bennett – who addressed me as 'Canon' – when admiring the OBE her late husband, a Merchant Navy captain had won for bravery after his ship was torpedoed during the war, while he was listening to their daughter in *The Archers* on the radio.

Damfield Lane, c. 1900. In 1668 Humphries Webster was the headmaster of the first school in Maghull, situated in School Lane, which later became farmworkers' cottages. A new school was started in 1830 in the small house which became the headmaster's house when the adjacent Maghull National School was built nine years later. By 1873 funds were raised to erect an extra storey. The Memorial School extension to commemorate the men of the parish who had been killed in the First World War was built following public subscription and opened by Jasper Wood on 30 June 1928.

Shortly before the Second World War the Alt Estate was started and in 1941 two shops were taken over in Dover Road as a junior school to cope with the number of evacuees in the area. Despite inadequate conditions, they remained in use until a new school was built in Moorhey Road for £62,000 in late 1947. The school was named after Mr S. Hudson, a native of Rugeley, in recognition of his work for education in Maghull. In April 1947 Mr W. Baird moved from Sale to become the headmaster of the new school where he would remain for several decades.

Four

Transport

By the 1950s almost the only trade on the canal through Maghull from Liverpool was to
Ainscough's Mill at Burscough.

Above: Hall Lane, Maghull. There were fifty-four wooden swing bridges across the Leeds to Liverpool canal, of which four were in Maghull. The Horse and Jockey, typical of the many canal beer houses, stood beside Hall Lane Bridge until it closed down before the last war. The small cottages behind were built for canal workers and the Coronation Cottages beyond were built to commemorate the coronation of King Edward VII in 1902. The children of Lydiate were given a crested china mug to commemorate the new king.

Left: Before public transport became readily available, the surrounding villages and farms relied upon delivery men to supply them. George Allin and his son Eddie stand outside the Kings Arms, Haskayne, in about 1916. They worked for Liptrots, a baker and general dealer situated behind the Running Horses in Lydiate, and took a different route each day to cover the district from Maghull to Great Altcar and Scarisbrick. Eddie Allin gave me the first group of local photographs to spark my interest in the history of the area.

Lollies Bridge. A canal maintenance unit led by a steamer barge passes towards Maghull. During the 1860s over one million tons of coal passed under this bridge bound for Liverpool whilst an important return cargo was manure for the local fields. There were several wharves, especially in Maghull, which also loaded vegetables. Also in Maghull were stables for canal horses and Lydiate had a small boatyard, which is now covered by the Moorings Estate.

Damfield Lane. Whilst vital to the economy of the area the canal has its dangers. Not only did several local residents drown after slipping from the unlit towpath, but on occasions the canal burst its banks, especially near Hall Lane. During the 1950s Damfield Lane, which took its name from the large field through which the Whinny Brook runs, was badly flooded outside the Coronation Cottages, to the great interest of these schoolboys.

Northway, 1951. This peaceful view of Northway looking toward St Andrew's church would be changed within a few years. Having developed through its position on the canal, railway and turnpike, Maghull would be affected dramatically by the motor car. In the thirties local councillors pleaded for a by-pass but Northway struggled to cope with increasing traffic from the new estates travelling to Liverpool until a dual carriageway was opened in 1963.

Hall Lane, Maghull, c. 1953. The Whinny Brook rises in Maghull Moss and flows past Hall Lane to join Maghull Brook behind the Meadows Hotel. A small, controlled stream today, it was once of importance but always threatened to burst its banks as it did in the early 1950s at the junction of Hall Lane and Northway, trapping a delivery van. An ancient water mill was situated on a small stream running through the nearby St George's School playing field.

Here the peaceful A59 winds from Old Roan Railway Bridge towards Woodend, forty years before motorway junctions and the Asda supermarket changed the view. During the last war the fields were used to store timber safely away from the Liverpool Docks. The Cheshire Lines Extension Railway Bridge evident in the middle distance was demolished in the 1960s.

During the 1930s it was decided to build new roads approaching and through Maghull and in particular, to ease the heavy traffic down Sefton Lane to Litherland. Northway, stretching from the Alt to the Sephton boundary, was opened in 1934 by Mr Hoare-Belisha, the Minister of Transport, whose name is recalled in the Belisha Beacon, and four years later it was extended from Dunnings Bridge to Litherland. Today, despite major road building the problem with Sefton Lane traffic persists.

Lydiate Station on the Southport and Cheshire Lines Extension Railway from Aintree to Southport was opened on 1 September 1884 but, having closed for a short while during the First World War, it finally closed completely in 1952 due to a lack of trade. Only the modernised station cottages remain, but the route of the line is now used as part of the Cheshire Lines Path which leads eventually to Hull.

Maghull Station, *c.* 1910. Could the directors of the Liverpool–Ormskirk–Preston railway have imagined the impact their plans would have upon Maghull? Within months of the opening of Maghull Station in April 1849, many new impressive houses were built near the station. Henry Poyser from Derbyshire was described as the railway clerk and station man and Esther Rainford, a widow from the Isle of Man, was the landlady of the new Railway Inn which would shortly be renamed the Mogul.

Sefton Lane. The site of the Sefton and Maghull Station on the Southport and Cheshire Lines Extension Railway is now covered by the Maghull Industrial Estate, although the bridge over the railway lines still exists. It was a popular station for skaters coming to the frozen fields flooded by the River Alt and Litherland's picnic fields near Sefton, but the line failed financially. During the late 1940s Maghull Town Council pleaded for more commuter trains to Southport but the committee was unable to provide these and the railway eventually closed. For a while the tracks were used for storing wagons and James Hilditch, a railway enthusiast, recalls lying in bed on winter nights and hearing the wagons clanking as the engines shunted them around.

Melling Lane. The American-born Samuel Cody made the first officially recognised flight in Great Britain in 1908. Two years later, amid great interest, he landed in the field in Melling Lane near the M58; the late Harry Anderton told me that as a young man he wrote his name on the aeroplane's fabric. Mr Cody was killed in 1913 while competing in a competition for seaplanes organised by the *Daily Mail*.

Liverpool Road South, *c.* 1935. A sight to excite any veteran car collector stands beside Wadsworth's Wharf with the British Workman's Cocoa Rooms in the background. The cars were owned by Mr Cobham the butcher. Lorries would line up to use the wharf and after the war, Mrs Lucy, a Maghull character, opened a sweet shop in the Cocoa Rooms. She was a tall, slim lady and I recall her sprinting across Northway when in her seventies, dodging the traffic.

Five

War and Peace

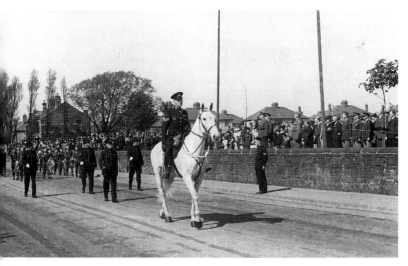

The Victory Parade past the King George V Recreation Field was a celebration of peace attended by almost all the residents of the two villages.

Green Lane, Maghull. The peace of Maghull was broken at 12.10 am on 28 July 1939 when a major explosion destroyed the Green Lane swing bridge. Eighty sticks of gelignite were bravely removed by Richard Dolan from an electricity pylon in a potato field on Thorn's Farm at Downholland. The police alleged that the explosives had been placed there by Terence O'Hanlon, aged 17, John Carney, aged 25 and Christopher Kenneally, aged 19, who were all Irishmen and admitted to being members of the Irish Republican Army.

By the outbreak of war in September 1939, the air raid wardens had trained for eighteen months, had issued a respirator to every resident and found emergency accommodation for air raid victims. Mr W. Higham, the headmaster of St Andrew's School, was the Chief ARP warden for West Lancashire. Maghull was divided into eighteen sectors, each with six wardens, and this group met in the bathroom of the Smiths' home at No. 199 Liverpool Road South. Their duties were to maintain the black-out, check gas masks, billet evacuees, issue ear plugs and train the Fire Guard. Fortunately very few bombs fell in the area and all landed on open ground.

The Leeds and Liverpool Canal was designated as a defence line should the Germans invade from the coast. There was a pill box at most local bridges and some were built by local builder Bill Kenney in 1940. The building with the damaged roof is a pill box, camouflaged as a cottage, near Coronation Cottages in Damfield Lane, as it appeared in 1951. It was demolished some thirty years later but there are still four pill boxes remaining: a rare double structure at Durant Cottages, two at Hall Lane and Green Lane in Maghull, with an excellent example at Billy's Bridge in Lydiate.

Many local men signed on at local police stations following Anthony Eden's broadcast announcing the formation of Local Defence Volunteers – later the Home Guard – on 14 May 1940. Captain John Atherton MC was appointed Commander of the 73rd Battalion County of Lancaster Home Guard with his headquarters at High Pastures in Maghull. Company headquarters in Maghull were located at the nearby Sayers' shop and at St George's church hall. The group in Sayers' shop are, standing from left to right: ? Copple, ? Leather, Walter Cannell, ? Lucy, ? Schofield. Sitting: Lieutenant Aspinall, Bill Cannell.

'C' Company under the command of Major R. Owen had its headquarters at the Memorial Hall in Lydiate and consisted of three patrols. At the start of the war the hall was manned most nights and patrols guarded road blocks leading from the coast and patrolled the open fields. Originally local volunteers A. Bowers, C. Rimmer and R. Boyer would place stops in the canal during air-raids lest the canal embankment broke, but this was taken over by 'C' Company at Jacksons Bridge and Downholland. After the war the War Office paid for a new dance floor at the hall to replace that damaged by the Home Guard.

Southport Road. Anti-tank blocks were placed at inland stop lines such as the canal and 'C' company are seen laying blocks at Lollies Bridge. In the central socket a barbed wire picket post would be placed. There are also some original blocks on the path at Billy's Bridge. There would be other defences such as anti-tank trenches nearby, and the new wall seems to be part of the defences.

Southport Road. Road blocks could also include moveable road barriers of several varieties. These at Lollies Bridge consisted of steel poles and the sockets are still present under the roadway. They are being inspected by Lt-Col. J.S. Atherton MC, with Capt. L. Brownlee and Lt Lionel Balmer of 'C' Company. Lt-Col. Atherton was awarded the Military Cross for bravery in the First World War and was an Aughton businessman.

The 73rd Battalion practiced shooting at Altcar Rifle Range at weekends but they also had a range at Bickerstaffe Colliery, under the control of Lt J. Ball, who was very impressed with the battalion's standard. Various forms of weapons were used, as were anti-tank bombs. Lt-Col. Atherton tried his skills with a Bren gun at Altcar.

Dr Reginald Burrows moved to Maghull from Ireland in the 1920s and was a respected general practitioner and medical officer at the Epileptic Homes. A stalwart of the Home Guard, Captain Burrows is seen with the First Aid Party. There was a First Aid Party Post in the Deyes Lane cricket pavilion consisting of sixteen men and six women with only one ambulance but several cars. In March 1941, two members, Mrs Dykins and Mrs McCreavy, were presented with OBEs at Buckingham Palace for bravery when they drove their patients during an air raid at Thornton.

Right: Captain Reginald Burrows was a very talented musician and as well as his medical duties, he led the Home Guard Band. He is seen at the back of the band having just passed Rosslyn Avenue on their way to St Andrew's church for a service conducted by Canon H. Frazer, one of the four battalion chaplains. Buried in the churchyard is Volunteer W.H. Grainger of the 89th County of Lancaster Home Guard from Hounslow, who died on 21 June 1941 aged 44 years.

Below: Marching proudly along Hall Lane after the Drum Head service on 24 May 1942, which the whole battalion attended, is Maghull 'A' Company with Lt-Col. John Atherton taking the salute. Lt E. Aspinall, a local builder, is seen in front of the policeman with his wife Edith standing amongst the guests. It is believed that the cine photographer was a captain from a local anti-aircraft unit and his film would be a treasure today. As the threat of invasion lessened, members became less enthusiastic and the Home Guard was disbanded in November 1944. Each member received a letter of gratitude from Major General G. Waterhouse, the District Commander.

In June 1941 three sites in Maghull, with Pygons Hill in Lydiate, were requisitioned for huts to acommodate 4,000 homeless Bootle residents. Some single men occupied the Deyes Lane Camp but they were all occupied by American troops in 1942. Polish forces later moved into the Damfield Lane site and in 1947 the Deyes Lane Camp became No.8 Families Camp for soldiers and their families, especially from India. On closure, several families were rehoused in Moorhey Road in 1959 where they still live.

Like many servicemen George Parkinson, a veteran of Monte Cassino, returned home and married a local girl. They moved into the Brookfield Estate: 'It was a tin hut and very noisy in the rain and hail showers but it was home to us, with a small coal fired stove in the living room and like living in the country, with a garden of my own growing my own flowers and vegetables; it was out of this world'. Pamela Parkinson aged 3 is enjoying playing in the garden.

Hall Lane, Maghull. The Maghull branch of the British Legion was formed in 1943 and members met in pubs and their homes before buying the Salem chapel. The branch received its standard at an impressive Drum Head service on King George V Recreation Field on 7 May 1944. The salute was taken by their president, Lord Sefton, with Lt-Col. W. Gildersleeves, an American Army officer, and Canon H. Frazer behind him. The parade is led by the authoritarian Inspector Philpott who worked in Maghull for many years before being promoted to Bury in 1946, and the standard is carried by Mr Thompson. The Salem chapel was demolished and a new building was opened by Lord and Lady Sefton in 1959.

In 1942 permission was given for Italian prisoners of war to be employed on farms. They either lived at the hostel in Aughton or on the farm, as seen at Shaw's farm in Pilling Lane, being visited by relatives after the war. The farmer paid the government 48s less 21s for accommodation whilst the unskilled POWs received only 3 farthings per hour with some pocket money. Their fraternizing with local girls caused unrest amongst the villagers, especially the young men. German prisoners of war replaced the Italians and stayed for some years after 1945 before repatriation. Not all of the POWs returned home because some married local girls and raised families here. Some, such as Italian Ginepro Salgari, have returned to visit their old friends.

The parishioners who died during the First World War were commemorated in Maghull by the construction of the Memorial School and a brass plaque under the cross at St George's church and in Lydiate, by a memorial in Our Lady's churchyard and a plaque in St Thomas's church. Those who returned safely were given a medal by the parish council. In 1944 a war memorial was proposed and two years later the Revd Leslie Hart requested names of fallen Maghull residents for two memorial tablets under a lychgate at a cost of about £300. The dedication ceremony in honour of the one woman, Marjorie Ellis, and sixty-one men who gave their lives took place in August 1952. The standard bearer was Norman Townley and the group included Joe Fay, Jim Clensey, Jim Roberts, A. Glenn, Revd Hart and Mr H. Stafford-Moreton.

Sefton Lane, c. 1955. During the last war the area of Sefton Drive was used to store valuable timber from Liverpool. After the Territorial Army was formed the Royal Scottish Battery and No.525 Light Anti-Aircraft and Search Light Regiment, Royal Artillery, occupied the site with regular weekly training. Many local men joined the unit after their National Service. In 1961 a small housing estate was built on the site. The small building on the right would develop into the large factory which became a major local employer but is today redundant, and its unforgettable smell is no longer part of Maghull life.

Foxhouse Lane, 1951. The temporary Housing Act in 1944 permitted the building of new homes and a site in Highfield Park was requisitioned for forty-six houses. They were manufactured in Hull by Tarron and the first ten were ready in July 1946 at a weekly rent of 10s amidst an outcry that they were not all available for Maghull families. Recently the temporary homes were replaced but Hal Birch, a former Lancaster wireless operator with No. 149 (East India) squadron and a senior nurse at Moss Side Hospital, lives with his wife in the last remaining original pre-fabricated home.

Liverpool Road South. Arriving in late 1942 the American soldiers had an immediate impact upon Maghull and the police had to close Maghull Station to keep young ladies from Liverpool away as well as stopping fights in local pubs. Great efforts were made to make them feel at home with social evenings and invitations to homes which led to much local gossip. The troops were visited by Mrs Eleanor Roosevelt and, it is said, Joe Louis the boxer.

Liverpool Road South. James Peacock was one of five officers with 3989QM Truck Company of Transportation Corps with 120 black soldiers. He wrote that there were problems with adjustment to all white 'Maghullians'. Travelling mainly to the docks the company had constant convoys fetching supplies and personnel throughout the United Kingdom. They left Maghull on 2 June 1944 for a camp near Hereford to prepare to transport troops to Southampton for D-Day but were not needed. They finally left Maghull to cross the Channel on 1 July – the first time James could discard his 'longies for GI undershorts'.

Liverpool Road South. The streets were lined with crowds for the large Victory Parade which included every branch of the services and the civil defence forces including the police, air raid wardens, first aid workers and national fire services. On VE Day there was a service of thanksgiving at King George V Recreation Field with several streets having parties. Mrs Covell of Claremont Avenue wrote to her husband Sydney that 'they rigged up lights on the telegraph pole, made a wooden stage for artists and had dancing to a piano which was brought from one of the houses'.

King George V Recreation Field. At the outbreak of war the field and Mr Boyer's pavilions were taken over by the 8th Irish King's Liverpool Regiment. Public air raid shelters were eventually built on the field, in schools and in some roads. During the Liverpool *Blitz* Maghull and Lydiate were crowded every night with evacuees sleeping in the schools and church buildings. A small children's hospital was opened in the Jehovah's Witness chapel in Hall Lane for the evacuees under the care of Dr Burrows and two nurses. Many evacuees lived in the area for several years, although not always happily, and may be amongst the crowd seen here enjoying the Victory Parade.

At the 1946 Remembrance Day Service at St Thomas's church, Lydiate, a Book of Remembrance and Pedestal Stool were dedicated. The names of the fallen were read out by churchwarden Robert Allin and the desk unveiled by William Postage, who had written the book. Ft Lt James Mullaney of No. 83 Squadron returned to Lydiate after the war having spent six months as a prisoner of war, but later died from an illness contracted whilst in captivity. Almost fifty years later, due to the efforts of his brother Tony and the co-operation of the church, Jimmy Mullaney's name was added to the memorial plaque and at a most touching Rememberance Day Service, attended by many Lydiate residents who remembered him as a young man, his name was read from the Book of Rememberance.

John Underwood of Rose Cottage, Lydiate, joined the RAF before the Second World War and by 1942 was a flight engineer sergeant with No. 214 Squadron flying Stirling bombers from Stradishall. On 2 July pilots Sgt T. Palmer and his crew took off with Wg Cdr K. Knocker to bomb Bremen. Over the northern Dutch coast they were shot down by a night fighter and all killed. The crew were buried in Westernieland Cemetery at Groningen. Kenneth Knocker's mother, the Baroness de T'Serclaes, wrote to each family and arranged for a wreath to be laid on the graves every year. Many local men are buried overseas including Roy Worthington of Lydiate, who died in a Japanese POW camp.

Six

Medical

Moss Side Hospital is internationally recognised for its research into the recognition and treatment of shell shock in the First World War.

Moss Side House, c. 1867. Thomas Harrison, an African merchant, moved from Liverpool to the new Moss Side House that he had built in Park Lane. The family later had financial problems and the large estate was sold in 1878 to the Liverpool Select Vestry for use as a convalescent home for workhouse children. In 1910 they started to build an epileptic colony but before it was finished the Lunacy Board of Control purchased the building in 1914 for £64,000.

Above: Moss Side House, *c.* 1867. The Harrison family constructed a beautiful garden with tree-lined paths and an ornamental lake with a grotto, which has hardly changed in appearance over 140 years. Local folklore states that when the lake was drained after the First World War, numerous weapons were found on the bed.

Right: The hospital became a Red Cross Hospital for shell shocked soldiers and the first twenty patients arrived on 7 December 1914. The nurses were members of the Royal Army Medical Corps but the hospital relied increasingly upon female nursing and domestic staff from all parts of the country. These young ladies are sitting around the ornamental lake as the Harrison daughters did fifty years before. During the First World War 3,138 soldiers were treated at Moss Side.

In May 1915 Dr Ronald Rows was transferred from Lancaster to the Red Cross Military Hospital at Maghull to become medical superintendant where he had a major influence upon the treatment of shell shock. He brought together a team of outstanding workers including, from left to right: Dr William Brown, Dr W. Rivers and Dr Elliot Smith. Rivers became perhaps the most famous 'shell shock doctor' in the First World War following his treatment of Siegfried Sassoon at Craiglockhart Hospital in Edinburgh. Later in the war small groups of medical officers attended courses at the hospital and most later obtained senior posts in psychiatry; through their influence they changed the face of British psychiatry. This led to a more enlightened view in the management of shell shock in the Second World War and has led to the understanding of post-traumatic stress disorder.

Right: Foxhouse Lane, *c.* 1918. Harry Cox was born at Leamington Spa and worked as a nurse at Knowle Mental Hospital before joining the Royal Army Medical Corps in 1914 when he was immediately posted to Moss Side, where he would meet his future wife. He remained at the hospital until 1920 when he was transferred to Rampton Hospital. Harry is seen standing in front of George Cross at the Red House public house with his friend James Kenna. The girl is George's granddaughter and her father Sam Rogers was the next landlord. Years later Harry's son, Harry junior, would return to work at Moss Side Hospital.

Below: The Ministry of Pensions used the 256 bed hospital for the treatment of former soldiers until 1933, when the Board of Control had to take over the hospital due to overcrowding at Rampton and transferred 100 patients. The soldiers in their distinctive blue uniforms had become a familiar sight in Maghull and were transferred to Mossley Hill Hospital. Moss Side and Rampton hospitals worked as one unit and staff were transferred as necessary, causing some distress.

MINISTRY OF PENSIONS, MAGHULL.

Left: Every effort was made to teach the patients useful skills but the hostel had diffculty finding suitable daily employment for patients outside the hospital. The local community had close links with the hospital and donated equipment as well as entertaining the patients. In 1944 a new east wing was opened and the hospital became very busy, including teaching nursing staff. Eventually the buildings of the original hospital became inadequate and after patients were moved to the adjacent Park Lane Hospital, the hospital closed in 1995.

Below: Park Lane, Maghull, 1960. The Bootle Corporation bought land in Park Lane in 1910 for the construction of an emergency smallpox hospital but in 1914 opened the hospital for the treatment of pulmonary tuberculosis patients. Many present local residents spent several months in the hospital and recall that on the weekend visiting day, they would wander around the country lanes with their visitors before they caught the bus back to Bootle. The last tuberculosis patients left in 1956 and it became Maghull Hospital for long-stay geriatric patients. However, the building became unsafe and closed on 28 February 1970, to be later demolished.

"QUARRY BROOK" ESTATE, MAGHULL

Comprising the Detached Residences " QUARRY BROOK " and " THE OLD HOUSE " also a Cottage let on a controlled tenancy and a total area of land extending to nearly 13 acres.

Conveniently situated within eight miles of Liverpool and about five minutes' walk from Maghull Station, on main L.M.S. electric line between Liverpool and Ormskirk.

TO BE OFFERED FOR

SALE BY AUCTION

By H. H. & J. ROBINSON, F.A.I.

On WEDNESDAY, 22ND MAY, 1946

AT 2-30 P.M. AT

The Property Exchange, 14 Cook Street, Liverpool

(Subject to Conditions of Sale and unless Previously Sold)

Solicitors : MESSRS. LAYTON & CO., 24 Chapel Street, Liverpool 3.
Auctioneers : H. H. & J. ROBINSON, F.A.I., 42 Castle Street, Liverpool 2. CENTRAL 6727
and at 117 South Road, Waterloo. WAT. 529.

Hall Lane. The original Quarry Brook in Hall Lane was replaced by this building which is now a Sisters of Mercy convent. William Vestey, who pioneered the transport of frozen meat from South America using his Blue Star Line ships, lived there before becoming the first Lord Vestey and Frank Hornby of Meccano fame lived there after him. During the First World War the building was used for the treatment of officers suffering from shell shock by doctors from Moss Side Hospital and in the last war as an officer's mess. In June 1946 the Sisters, who had a private school in Kennessee House, bought the estate from the Hornby family and established a larger school which developed into Maricourt School.

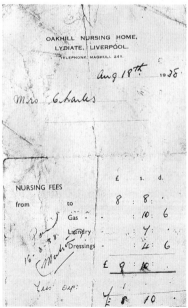

OAKHILL NURSING HOME,
LYDIATE, LIVERPOOL.
TELEPHONE: MAGHULL 241.

Aug 18th 1938

Mrs G Charles

	£	s.	d.
NURSING FEES			
from to	8	8	
Gas -		10	6
Laundry -		4	
Dressings -		4	6
£	9	10	

Above: Between the wars several nursing homes, some especially for obstetrics, were opened and had close links to individual general practitioners. Oakhill House in Liverpool Road was used by Dr Burrows. Tragically a patient died there in 1938 and shortly afterwards the nursing home closed and the State Insurance Company from Liverpool moved in. Miss Millicent Holme started work there as a clerk in April 1940, working in a hut in the garden, and recalls that it was a beautiful building. Eventually used by an electricity company, it was demolished around 1950.

Left: Although there were some insurance schemes that could be used for medical treatment, generally a fee was involved. This bill to Mrs Charles is for the delivery of her daughter Betty, who appears in the Lydiate Rose Queen photographs.

The Manor House Home for Epileptics was opened in 1888 as 'the first epileptic home in England' following the efforts of some Liverpool philanthropists. The second home was opened in 1894 and named after Henry Cox, a Liverpool merchant, who offered anonymously to found a small hospital in the open country as suggested by Dr William Alexander, a Rodney Street surgeon, 'where work, treatment, education and all good influences could be brought to bear' on the patients. After steady growth over the decades the Maghull Homes consisted of eleven villas, a school, workshops and social centres covering a large part of the town, but in recent years several of the buildings have been put to different uses.

Maghull Homes, c. 1930. Many local dignitaries became involved with the Homes and the Lord Mayor of Liverpool was appointed president. Sporting activities were encouraged and the highlight of the year was the sports day when over 100 prizes were awarded. The first medical officer was Dr Gordon, followed by his partner Dr Nesbitt and then Dr Burrows, standing at the right, who gave forty years dedicated service to the Homes.

Left: The local doctors prescribed their own medicines until Norman Radcliffe opened the first chemists shop in Maghull, in Station Road in 1930, before opening a second shop opposite the Meadows in the 1940s. Jack Hesketh and John Walker met whilst serving in the Army and after the war opened a shop at No. 89 Liverpool Road South, which eventually became Boydell and Keating's. As the National Health Service expanded there were at one time nine chemists shops in the district.

Below: Dr Monica Hurst was one of the most popular general practitioners in the area working from her surgery Broadwood House, near the Alt Estate. Monica was a geography teacher before becoming a doctor in 1935 when she qualified with a gold medal. Born in St Helens, she loved listening to her patients' broad Lancashire accents and would lie in bed listening to the horses and wagons heading for the Liverpool markets. Following her retirement in 1988 she lived at Ince Blundell Nursing Home and her practice was taken over by Dr Peter Gregson.

Seven

Sports and Leisure

The Maghull Conservative Club was opened on 11 May 1912 by the Rt Hon Arthur Stanley MP and the bowling green was open by 1914. During the two World Wars the club opened its doors to the officers, including the Americans stationed in the district, and entertained wounded soldiers.

Maghull Football Club was formed in 1921 and later joined the I. Zingari Alliance, winning the Alliance Cup and championship in 1924/5. They played their home games at Hurst Park near Maghull Station. Back row from left to right: E. Cross, F. Eastham, J. Kirby, G. Smith, J. Cropper, W. Watson, A. Cropper, W. Sephton, H. Ledger, -?-, J. Sephton, A. Cross, H. Gard, W. Prescot. Front row: referee, -?-, J. Gard, W. Turner (chairman), -?-, F. Haskayne, S. Pimbley, W. Cairns.

In 1949 Maghull Football Club won the Lancashire Amateur Cup by defeating Manchester University at Goodison Park. The successful team in their famous blue and white hooped shirts were, back row, from left to right: John Travis, Harry Bayliss, Tom Barlow, Ted Anderton, Stan Anderton, Jack Barcas. Front row: Les Rigby, Tommy Lowe, Bill Ibbotson, Dick Wood, Stan Eastham, George Brazier. The club played on the Pimbley Recreation Ground from 1928 before moving to the Old Hall Playing Field after the war and changing in the Travellers Rest Inn.

The celebration of King George V's Silver Jubilee took place on 6 May 1935 on Boyers Field. It was planned to present a flag pole and Union Jack to all the schools in Maghull including the Epileptic Homes School as a permanent record of the event. Councillor James Longridge is seen addressing the crown with John Broadbent, who seemed to be the Honourary Organising Secretary of all celebrations, standing at the far right. Broadbent House, the warden-controlled sheltered accommodation, is named after him in honour of his achievements.

After organising the celebrations for the 1937 Coronation on the premises of the Maghull Catering Company in Hall Lane, Councillor John Broadbent was presented with a clock by James Longridge. Leading the cheers is H. Stafford Moreton, with the music provided by the Birkenhead Town Silver Band conducted by Arthur Clarke. They had a long day, playing for eight hours, concluding with dance music in the evening. Arrangements were made to broadcast the King's message to the Empire at the celebrations.

CORONATION. 1937.
THE. LADS. OF. THE. VILLIAGE.
MAGHULL.

The sports events included every kind of race for children of all ages, finishing with pillow fighting, tilting the bucket and, intriguingly, the honeymoon race! The 'Boys at the Village' played a comic football match against 'Real Players' from the United Sports Club. The Boys team was, T. Wilson, B. Kirkham, T. Jones, E. Appleton, J. Harrison, R. Rogers, J. Eastham, E. Rimmer, J. Pope, S. Ward, E. de Abaituea. A warning in the programme banned spectators from tempting the players with refreshments of any sort.

This postcard of 22 June 1912 reads: 'Dear Min, If you would care to go that walk tomorrow Sunday I will be at the corner of Derby Lane by the Bank, at 7.15, I'll wait about quarter of an hour. I have just been for a run to Southport on the bike and all went well till I got as far as this bridge on my way home and then a delightful little stone made a beautiful round square hole in my front tyre so I thought I would buy a postcard of the spot. From Geo.'

Tommy Barnes, the local blacksmith, sought his relaxation away from the area and built a caravan which he called Dinky Nest in 1929. The first trip was to Ross-on-Wye, driving in his pride and joy, a three-year-old Peugeot 6.5 hp motor car. His wife Pauline is perhaps more smartly dressed than the modern caravaner. Their later trips would include daughter Doris, with baby son Alan in a cradle.

The first bowling club in Maghull was at the Mogul and members are seen here at a prize day. The bowling green was sold in November 1959 for £8,900 – the equivalent of a record £11,000 per acre – to a London development company. In 1939 the newly-built Meadows Hotel formed a 'bowling club and by August 1940 had a new green ready but on September 7 a German bomb fell', leaving a huge crater right in the centre which was not repaired until 1946, although the green was not ready for use for some years. Eventually, the demands of modern life led to the green being replaced by a car park – the fate which recently befell the Alt Park Hotel bowling green.

The Lydiate Girls Club was started in 1928 and gave pensioners a New Year's Day party every year, except during the Second World War, until 1988 when Charlie Rigby of The Scotch Piper took over the arrangements. The photograph, taken after a procession through Ormskirk in 1928 shows standing, from left to right: Nancy Leyland, May Kirkham, Ida Lowe, Doris Harper, Alice Rimmer, Myra Scarisbrick, Ada Coles. Sitting: Edith Holme, Josie Royden, Rita Quilliam, Dolly Drew, Winnie Heighway, Connie Asquith, Kathleen Holme. At the front: Edna Quilliam.

During the Second World War the government put forward suggestions for 'holidays at home' and the Maghull Gala Committee proposed a queen to reign on the Gala Day, held on the August Bank Holiday Monday. Maureen Davies was the first Rose Queen in 1943 and the gala grew in stature and popularity. Queen Jean Melville is seen with her retinue on the King George V Field in 1947, when the popular Morris Dancing competition was held for the first time.

Above: The Lydiate Rose Queen procession passes St Thomas's School in about 1948 with the Ropery in the background. The two girls, third and fourth from the left, are Betty Charles and Laura Gatley with Beryl Blundell and Barbara Bell leading.

Right: Frances Gatley, the four-year-old sister of Laura, won the fancy dress competition in 1950 but Darkie, the Kerry blue family pet seems to find something else more interesting.

Laura Gatley was the Lydiate Rose Queen in 1950 with Betty Charles and Doreen Garner as her ladies-in-waiting. The Court Ladies are Dorothy Bond, Stephanie Wood and Betty Leyland with Alan Shaw the Crown Bearer. It was a lovely day and Rose Queens from the surrounding villages joined in the celebrations on the field behind the parish hall.

Samuel Boyer of Maghull Old Hall formed the Maghull Catering Company and entertained parties in huts on his land, which is now the site of Maghull Town Hall. Most parties came from Liverpool, as did the Tetlow Methodist chapel outing, and such visits would be the first introduction to Maghull for several future residents.

The Maghull Moorland Social Club was a very active organisation and members met at Hudson School. In 1953 members and friends made a trip to Trentham Gardens to celebrate the coronation. Could they have imagined then that one young lady, Rhona Christian, would become Mayor of Maghull?

Left: There were numerous public houses in Maghull and Lydiate, some of which are now over two centuries old. Several such as the Millers Arms, the Travellers Rest, the Horse and Jockey and the Farmers Arms have long gone. Most stood on the turnpike route but later developed a social use as a place of gathering for events including dances, public meetings and even inquests. The Coach and Horses closed in 1961 when a new hotel was opened next door on the site of Woodland Mount.

Below: The old Coach and Horses is fondly remembered but the local press reported that 'it seemed that the regulars would not miss the open fire in a tiny grate that flutters behind the bar. Regulars said "you won't find anybody here as'll miss anything". Said a patron of more years than he cared to remember that they could hardly wait for the new pub to open.'

Mr Collier, a popular teacher at Hudson School, wrote and produced a musical about Richard the Lionheart. His class performed the play at the school with Phillip Rowlands as King Richard in 1952. Rhona Simon recalls that the knights' chain-mail was knitted from old dish cloths and painted silver. Mr Collier left to become a headmaster in Litherland.

Johnny Carey, the distinguished Irish international footballer, was manager at Everton Football Club for three years from 1968 until his dismissal under notorious circumstances. Mr Tom Nuttall of Sefton Lane was an Everton director and could have arranged this visit by Mr Carey, who is seen flanked by local personalities Harry Prescott, Douglas Grieg, H. Stafford Moreton and John Broadbent.

The Maghull Cricket Club was formed in 1926 after local farmer John Pimbley, in the front row, donated 6 acres of land in Deyes Lane as a sports field and £2,000 to build a pavilion. Lord Vestey performed the opening on 11 June 1927 and stands behind Mr Pimbley with Mrs Frank Hornby and Lady Vestey sitting on the left. The trustees presented John Pimbley with an inscribed silver salver and after a cricket match between Maghull and an Ormskirk XI, the public had a free tea.

DATE 25/7/38 Maghull V M.T.S.	GROUND		
BATSMEN INNINGS OF M.T.S.	**HOW OUT**	**BOWLER**	
1 R. Runcie	BOWLED	BOOTH	
2 A Wooldridge	Cᵗ (Brown)	BOOTH	
3 J. Robinson	LBW	CLEMENTS	
4 J. Gardner	LBW	BOOTH	
5 D. Winter	BOWLED	CLEMENTS	
6 G. Blackwood	NOT	OUT	
7 C. Kelsey	RUN	OUT	
8 J. Cornwell	NOT	OUT	
9 J. Lamb			
10 S. Jones	DID NOT BAT		
11 J. Alcock	122 for 6		
WIDES		TOTAL EXTRAS	
BYES	2.41		
LEG BYES	1	7	TOTAL
NO BALLS			
FALL OF WICKETS 1 27 2 32 3 32 4 45 5 45 6 115 7 8 9 10	RESULT: DRAWN GAME		

BOWLERS	RUNS AS SCORED	WIDES	NO BALLS	OVERS	MDNL	RUNS	WKTS
W. Clements				10	1	38	2
F. Booth				12	2	29	3
G. Croasker				5	2	11	

Stan Brown, a local man, was an outstanding sportsman and in the 1930s was captain of both Maghull Football and Maghull Cricket Clubs. In 1938 he scored a century which included nineteen fours, against Merchant Taylors School. The school's opening batsman, Robert Runcie, later became the Archbishop of Canterbury and Stan sent him a copy of the score sheet.

Eight

Around the District

School group, Haskayne School, c. 1890

Above: Ince is first mentioned in the Domesday Book as 'Hinne', meaning island, and was associated with the Blundell family from the twelfth century. The village smithy stood opposite the sign post which, surprisingly in such a peaceful scene, asks drivers to drive slowly.

Left: The new Ince Hall was completed in 1750 and land was exchanged with Lord Sefton so that the impressive park wall could be started in 1770, possibly as an employment relief scheme. The brick clay was dug from inside the park over six years and the pits became ornamental lakes. The young ladies seem to be standing near the road to Southport in about 1910 and may be domestic staff from the hall.

The road from Thornton to Ince Blundell, past the imposing Lion Gate guarding an entrance into the estate, before following the park wall towards the round priest's house and then on to the village. Before a Liverpool bus service arrived, villagers would walk to Crosby to catch a tram for the city.

Lydiate Lane, Thornton, c. 1930. The lane led towards the crossroads at the ancient Sefton Town but progress has now changed the scene beyond all recognition and the field on the right is now a playing field.

The road from Sefton Church to Thornton, originally past the rectory which was a large rambling Georgian building, which proved increasingly difficult to maintain; after the rector moved to the new rectory, it was taken over by squatters. It was demolished about thirty years ago.

Lunt Road, Sefton. The water from St Helen's Well was said to cure many ailments but its healing properties were probably due its coldness. The bottom was covered with pins by young folk who wished to know their marriage prospects, which were favoured if the pins fell pointing towards Sefton Church. The well was covered over by Mr Rimmer of Rose Cottage some years ago.

The River Alt was dammed at Dunnings Bridge in Maghull and the water of the mill dam flowed to Sefton Mill, said to have been built in 1595, although it is now demolished and the mill stream filled in.

Bridges Lane, Sefton, c. 1895. George Harrison took this unique photograph of the mill stream passing under Mill Bridge on the road from Sefton to Maghull. The bridge has now been demolished.

St Helen's church, Sefton, is one of the treasures of the district. Mainly built in the sixteenth century there is evidence of an earlier church. Amongst its treasures are the rich Gothic screen, wooden pews and the Molyneux family monuments. There is an unusual war memorial honouring not just the parishioners who died in the First World War, but also those who served and returned home safely. This rare print from around 1840 was discovered in a house and presented to the late Canon Yandell. Buried in the churchyard are John Sadler, a Liverpool inventor who discovered the process of transferring patterns to earthenware, and Flight Lieutenant George Storey, a fighter pilot who was killed in the Battle of Britain. Opposite the church on the moated site, which is still visible, was the ancient home of the Molyneux's which was finally dismantled in 1720.

Lunt Road, c. 1930. Lunt village was first mentioned in 1295 as 'Lund' when it was a hamlet of Sefton and became a village in its own right in 1624. Lunt Hall was at one time the residence of the curate of Sefton church. Before the last war the Berry family lived in the hall which, during the war, was used by Bootle Corporation for storage and fell into disrepair. After demolition only the gate posts remain.

John Johnson and John Cartwright, described as collectors from Great Crosby, seemed to have borrowed money from Luke Birches to build the Lunt Tithebarn in 1693. There is an unusual sculptured lintel stone over the flight of stone steps and in recent years the barn has been expertly converted into a dwelling.

Haskayne School was originally located in the old building near the present school which was opened on 29 August 1891. The children are playing different group games in front of the school.

School Lane, Haskayne. The Tyrer family from Bolton owned the cottages named after them, one of which was a mission in 1920. They were demolished to make way for modern bungalows in about 1957.

Right: Towards the end of the nineteenth century the Shacklady family farmed Downholland Hall. The elderly lady is Mrs Margaret Charles' Grandmother Shacklady who lived here with her sister. On the rising land beyond the nearby canal the Revd Gibson suggested there had been a small Roman outpost.

Below: The Scarisbrick Arms public house was rebuilt in 1899 and the landlord, Mr Waterson, stands in the doorway. Third from the left is Jack Shacklady, a farmer from Downholland Hall, with Richard Dolan next to him. The greatest day of the year was the Waterloo Cup Meeting when it seemed to the village children that all the local workers would go home drunk.

Broad Lane, Aughton. The Waggoners Inn closed in the mid 1960s when its licence was transferred to the Everest Hotel in Maghull. A typical country pub which served only beer, the narrow hall led to a men-only smoke room, a lounge and a small bar, with a serving hole, which contained an iron-frame Honky-Tonk piano where a young Rob Molyneux would play when home from boarding school under the watchful eye of the last landlords, Ronnie and Rita Knowles.

Liverpool Road, Aughton. The foundation stone taken from Aughton Delph, of Christ church, was laid in 1867 but due to financial problems it was ten years before the church was consecrated by Bishop Jacobson of Chester. The congregation could see the famous ship the *Great Eastern* leaving the Mersey.

Halsall Station on the Liverpool, Southport and Preston Junction Railway was opened in 1887 and finally closed in 1952. It was one of the stations used by 'Altcar Bob', which consisted of a small steam locomotive and single coach.

Halsall Rectory. This postcard dated 12 September 1910 reads: 'Dear Mother and Father, Arrived here Saturday afternoon. All are fairly well. Bert came by boat to within ? miles and then he met a postman who gave him a lift . Best regards, C.' The card was sent to Mr and Mrs Bowler, 87 Knowsley Road, Bootle.

Kings Arms Hotel, Haskayne, c. 1918. The three Sharrock brothers enjoy the comradeship of two friends on leave from the First World War. We can only imagine the horrors they may have experienced and wonder if they ever returned to their home village and the scattered farms amongst the rich flat fields of south west Lancashire, which may at first seem uninteresting, but which still have a fascinating story to tell to those who take up the challenge to scratch beneath the surface.

Acknowledgements

I am grateful to the following who have kindly provided me with photographs: Mr D. Moore, Mr D. Cropper, Mr R. Knowles, Mrs N. Yandell, Miss Mabel Holme, Miss Millicent Holme, Mrs M. Hayes, Mr P. Berry, Mr C. Bayliss, Mrs M. Charles, Mrs L. Singleton, Mr P. Culshaw, Mrs E Aspinall, Mrs J. Rothwell, Mrs P. Russell, Miss D. Barnes, Mrs Boyer, Mrs B. Rutherford, Mrs Tickle, Dr H. Hands, Mr J. Underwood, Mr A. Mullany, Mr R. Blundell, Mrs A. Dickinson, Mrs R. Simon, Mr B. Davis, Mr G. Parkinson, Mr H. Cox, Mrs H. Brown, Mr T. Harrison, Ashworth Hospital, *Ormskirk Advertiser*, *Liverpool Post and Echo*, Maghull Town Council and the late Mr E Allin, Revd Father Errity, Mr J. Whalley, Mrs E. Cobham, Mrs W. Martin, Mrs E. Appleton, Mr G. Swift, Mrs Smith, Mr and Mrs C. Currall and Mr W. Curran.

I am indebted to the many local residents who through their recollections have added to our knowledge of the history of the district. I am especially grateful to Sue Brigden for her many hours of typing and Denis Oates for his invaluable help in reproducing many of the photographs so expertly; without their help this book could not have been produced. Finally I wish to thank my wife Cathy for her constant encouragement and support.